For more laughs get these other LOL books now:

ISBN: 978-1642502343

Squeaky Clean Super Funny Knock Knock Jokes for Kidz

ISBN: 978-1642502367

Squeaky Clean Super Funny School Jokes for Kidz

ISBN: 978-1642502381

Squeaky Clean Super Funny Riddles for Kidz

SQUEAKY CLEAN SUPER FUNNY

JOKES!

for kidz

Craig Yoe

LOL!

mango

CORAL GABLES

Cover Design: Craig Yoe and Clizia Gussoni
Cover Photo/illustration: Craig Yoe
Layout & Design: Elina Diaz

For permission requests, please contact the publisher at:
Mango Publishing Group
2850 S Douglas Road, 2nd Floor
Coral Gables, FL 33134 USA
info@mango.bz

For special orders, quantity sales, course adoptions and corporate
sales, please email the publisher at sales@mango.bz. For trade and
wholesale sales, please contact Ingram Publisher Services at customer.
service@ingramcontent.com or +1.800.509.4887.

Squeaky Clean Super Funny Jokes for Kidz

Library of Congress Cataloging-in-Publication number: 2019954715
ISBN: (print) 978-1-64250-232-9 , (ebook) 978-1-64250-233-6
BISAC category code JUVENILE NONFICTION, Humor /
Jokes & Riddles

Printed in the United States of America

ROTFL!

Fuzzy: Why did the bear get cold?

Wuzzy: He was walking around with bear feet!

Mike: How do you stop a skunk from smelling?
Ike: Hold its nose!

Moe: When are boats cuddly?

Flo: When they hug the shore!

Why did the fish cross the road?

What road?!?!?

Q: Why did the wildcat get sent to the principal's office?

A: He was a cheetah! LOL!

The deli worker is thirty-six years old, five feet four inches tall and wears a size 8 ½ shoe. What does she weigh?

Cheese!

Nutty News!

Why didn't the turkey want dessert?

He was stuffed! :D

> ### Q: What did one light bulb say to the other light bulb?
> A: Let's go out tonight!

Sue: What song do frogs sing to each other once a year?

Stu: Hoppy birthday!

Milly: Why is a mouse little and gray?

Willy: If it was big and red it would be a barn! :P

Why don't ants ride bicycles?

Because they don't have thumbs to ring the bell!

Q: What's black and white and goes to pizza parlors?

A: Zebras that like pizza! ROTFL!

Batty Books!

Life on the River
By Rhoda Boat

You Can Do This!
By Cary Onn

Seeing the Wonders of the World
By Major Look

I Cured My Cravings
By Anida Berger

Helping the Poor
Linda Money

Solving Math Problems
By Adam Upp

Getting Exercise at Home
By Skip Rope

Chunks of Chuckles!

What did one candle say to the other candle?

These birthdays burn me up!

Iggy: How does a door feel after taking a bath?

Ziggy: Squeaky clean!

Kid lightning bug: I feel achy.

Papa lightening bug: Awww, it's probably just glowing pains!

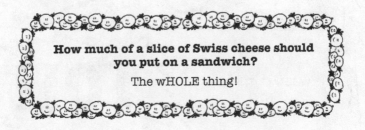

How much of a slice of Swiss cheese should you put on a sandwich?

The wHOLE thing!

Why do little pigs eat so much?

Because they want to make hogs of themselves!

14

Side Splitters!

Mom: Why couldn't the pancake go to school?

Dad: She had a waffle cold!

She: How do you keep an elephant from going through a keyhole?

He: Tie a knot in its tail! LOL!

When do birthday candles like to go to parties?
On the WICK-ends!

Q: Why did the horse take a bat to bed?

A: He wanted to hit the hay!

Where does a pig go when she's sick?

To the HOG-spital!

Jerry: Why did the homeowner buy a cow?
Teri: To MOO the lawn!

LOL!

Artie: What didn't the cow like about art class?

Smarty: Drawing flies! ;)

Why did the ocean keep the beach clean?

It wanted to be tide-y!

Mona: Why do you put a watch in the bank?

Lisa: To save time!

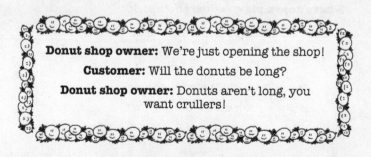

Donut shop owner: We're just opening the shop!

Customer: Will the donuts be long?

Donut shop owner: Donuts aren't long, you want crullers!

Fun and Games!

Q: Can I tell you a secret about peanut butter?

A: Yes, I promise I won't spread it around! HA-HA!

Customer: Waiter how long will my hotdog be?

Waiter: Five inches! :D

Why did the moth go to the light bulb?
It wanted some light entertainment!

Grandma: How do you make an egg chuckle?

Grandpa: Read him one of these yolks! HAHAHA!

Customer: Waiter! There's a footprint on my lunch!

Waiter: Sir, you said you wanted a ham sandwich and step on it!

What goes WOEM, WOEM, WOEM!?
A cat talking backwards!

What Do You Call...?!

WHAT DO YOU CALL a rhinoceros that wears a wig?

A wig-wearing rhinoceros!

Q: WHAT DO YOU CALL a man with a shovel?

A: Doug! ROTFL!

> **WHAT DO YOU CALL a very young chicken?**
> An egg.

WHAT DO YOU CALL two ice-cream scoops?

Ice-cream clones!

WHAT DO YOU CALL a chicken that can sing?

Hen-tertaining!

WHAT DO YOU CALL a camel without a hump?
A horse! :D

WHAT DO YOU CALL a baby gnu?

A gnu-bie!

Witty Bitties!

When's the best time to get a good deal on a thermometer?

In the winter, when they are lower!

Q: What do you get when an elephant jumps on your sidewalk with a pogo stick?

A: Big holes in your sidewalk!

What did the mama fork give the naughty baby fork?

Tyne out!

What's the worst thing to eat at the beach?
A SAND-wich. LOL!

Mona: I hope I can count on you!

Lisa: Sure, use my fingers!

What does the kid of a rooster and an owl say in the morning?

Cockle-doodle-whooo! ;)

Gorilla of My Dreams!

What do you call a boy with a five hundred-pound gorilla on his head?

Flat.

> **Hank:** What did the cow say when she got attacked by a gorilla?
>
> **Frank:** Nothing, cows can't talk!

Q: What time is it when you see a five hundred-pound gorilla?

A: Time to run!

What do you call a five hundred-pound gorilla in a locker?

Stuck!

How do you tell a five hundred-pound gorilla from a stinkbug?

I dunno!

A five hundred-pound gorilla looks nothing like a stinkbug!

Q: Why did the gorilla get sent to the principal's office?

A: He had a bad ape-titude.

Have You Heard This One?

Why were the glue and the scotch tape best friends?

They always stuck together!

> **Q:** Why did the cargo ship captain quit?
> **A:** She didn't like the pier pressure! ;)

What does a dog play in the school band?

The trom-bone! :D

> **Uncle:** What do you do if your dog chews this joke book?
>
> **Aunt:** Take the words out of her mouth!

What does a duck do when it flies upside down?

It quacks up! LOL!

Coach: Do you know what you need to do before you can become a good tennis player?

Boy: Become a good nine-is player?

Shirley You're Joking!

Sidney: If everyone drove a red car what would we have?

Shirley: A red car-nation!

Sidney: Why did the robin fly south for the winter?

Shirley: It didn't want to be a b-r-r-r-d!

Sidney: I want to buy a feather pillow!

Shirley: You'll need a down payment! :P

Sidney: What does a turtle use to call his friends?

Shirley: A shell phone!

Sidney: What kind of cheese do moths like?

Shirley: MOTHS-arella! LOL!

Silly Inventions

☺ A left-handed pencil!

☺ A right-handed spoon!

☺ A screen door for a submarine!

☺ A rubber crutch!

☺ A concrete lifeboat!

☺ A book on how to read!

Funny Bones!

Q: What is a reporter's favorite dessert?

A: An ice-cream scoop! :D

What did the farmer say when he saw the cows coming into the barn?

"There go the cows into the barn!"

Joan: What's orange and hangs on an apple tree branch?

John: A lost orange. ROTFL!

Izzy: What smells most at a perfume counter?

Dizzy: Your nose!

Sal: I heard baseball players aren't using bats any longer!

Val: Yeah, the bats are long enough now.

Load Up the Laughs!

English teacher: I cannot give you an A on your essay on marathon running.

Student: Why not?

English teacher: There were too many run-on sentences.

Kid: Why did you give me twelve quarters instead of three one-dollar bills for doing my chores?

Parent: Change is good for a person! ;)

How do you get rid of a dog's fleas?

You start from scratch!

Q: How do you fix broken pasta?

A: With tomato paste! LOL!

Brenda: Who's the strongest woman in the world?

Robin: A traffic cop. She can hold up many cars with one hand!

What kind of car does a cow drive?

A li-MOO!

Why do melons get married?

Because they cantaloupe!

Book Banter!

What to Do If You Feel Sick
By C. A. Dok

Curing a Split Personality
By Ima Nee and Ima Nee

How to Lose Weight
By Len Mete

Making Tasty Meals
By Carmen Getit

Dealing with Reality
By Faith DeMusic

Learning to Be Grateful
By Frank U. Verimuch

Seizing Opportunities
By Greta Lyff

Being Persistent
By Dawn Giveup

Greet with Greatness
By Hans Jive

Getting Your Fair Share
By Hanna Itover

How to Be a Painter
By Andrew Goode

Getting a Good Night's Sleep
By Earl Toobed

Making New Friends
By Bea Pal

Everybody's Important
By Evan Yu with Anna Me

Giving It Another Try!
By Celeste Time

Looney Laffs

Two robots were talking...

"U-8?"

"Yeah. U-2?"

> **He:** What driver never stops at stop signs?
> **She:** A screwdriver!

Why did the chicken swim across the sea?

To get to the other tide!

Q: Why did the poet stop writing?

A: He couldn't get much verse.

> **Beth:** What does an official say at the start of an insect race?
>
> **Seth:** One, two, BEE...go!

What does an official say at the start of a tree race?

One, two...wait a minute, trees can't race!

Laughing My Shelf Silly!

The Ultimate Diet Book
By Ima Hungry

How to Stop Robocalls
By Joan Calus

You Can Conquer All Your Fears!
By Ima Fraid

I Found Buried Treasure!
By Doug Deep

The End of My Troubles
By Gladys Over

Learning Good Manners!
By Hugo Furst

Squeaky Clean Super Funny Jokes
By Joe King

How to Be Popular
By Percy Nality

Keep on Moving
By Rollin Bie

How to Dress Sharp
By Luke Snappy

Reverse Name Game!

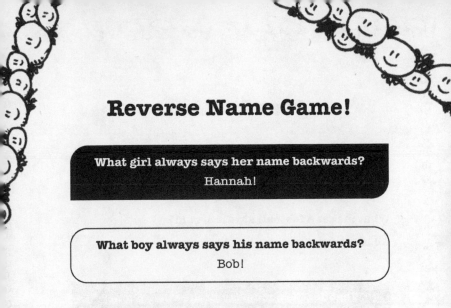

What girl always says her name backwards?
Hannah!

What boy always says his name backwards?
Bob!

Jest for Fun!

Phil: Why did the woodcutter take a break?

Jill: She had a splitting headache! ROTFL!

What makes a football stadium cold?

All of the fans!

What did the phone say to the other phone?
I hope you give me a ring!

Q: Why did the termite quit its job?

A: It was boring! :P

I Laugh a Good Book!

How to Succeed in Life
By Keith Ontrien

Standing Up to Bullies
By Julie Mealone

How to Be Patient
By Allen Goode-Tyme

Being a Good Friend
By Leon Mee

Getting to Where You Want to Be
By Haily Taxi

How to Pack a Suitcase
By Phil Idup

Cooking for a Big Party
By Ethan Alott

That's So Punny!

Why did Goldilocks enter the house in the woods?

She saw a sign, "bear left"!

What ten-letter word starts with gas?

Motorcycle! LOL!

Ned: Why was the owl silent?

Ed: It didn't give a hoot!

Q: What do you get when you cross ducks
with elephants?

A: Swimming trunks!

What did the goose say in the snowstorm?

I have people bumps!

Math Mirth!

A judge + a skater = Just-ice!

Dolphin + Cinderella = Glass flippers!

Pizza + rodents = Pie-rates!

Lawn mower + canoe = Mow, mow, mow your boat!

Ballet dancer + railroad = Tutu train!

Will: WHAT DO YOU CALL a bunk bed
with six levels?

Bill: A lot of bunk!

WHAT DO YOU CALL a skunk tossed with a pachyderm?

A SMELLY-phant!

WHAT DO YOU CALL twins that fall on the ice?

A: A pair of slippers! HAHAHAHA!

WHAT DO YOU CALL a spice on sale at the grocery store?

A good dill!

WHAT DO YOU CALL a tree in winter?

Tim-brrrr!

WHAT DO YOU CALL cool square rodents?

Mice cubes!

Funny Stuff!

Principal: Why did you quit teaching your history class?

Teacher: I didn't see any future in it!

I need some snoo.

What's snoo?

Nothing much. What's snoo with you?

Q: What's always behind the time?

A: The back of your watch!

What month are gorillas born in?
APE-ril!

Matty: What did the beach say to the waves?

Patty: SEA you later!

Harry: I failed my eye exam!

Mary: Why?

Harry: I thought I could do it with my eyes closed!

What's a frog's favorite food?

French flies!

What do you do before getting out of a car?

Get into it!

Silly Dillys

Ann: Why shouldn't you sleep at the edge of a cliff?

Dan: You might drop off!

Q: How are Attila the Hun and Henry the VIIIth similar?

A: They both have the same middle name!

A DEEP THOUGHT: A helicopter can fly, but a fly can't helicopter!

How did the sandwich get to the hospital?

In a HAM-bulance!

What's the capital of Kentucky?

K!

Why did a house have a thermometer on the wall?

It was homesick.

Morris: I want to be a stand-up comic, but I can't remember my lines!

Horace: You're choking!

Book Banter!

How to Break News Stories
By Justin Nao

Getting Fresh Air
By Hugo Owt

Safe Winter Driving
By I. C. Rhode

Scary Ghost Stories
By Tera Fied

Veggie Cooking
By Brock Lee

SHHHH at the Library!
By Cy Lent

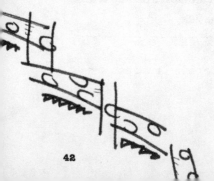

Monkey Business!

What would you call a team of monkeys if they won the World Series?

CHIMP-ions!

What's back, white, and red all over?
A zebra with a sunburn!

Hickory: Where do you find Florida?

Dickory: On a map!

What has lots of teeth but never bites?
A comb!

What kind of books do spoons like to read?

Stirring mysteries! LOL!

That's So Punny!

Uncle: What roof covers the biggest noisemaker?
Aunt: The roof of the mouth! :D

Why can't a Dalmatian play hide and seek?

Because she's always spotted!

When does a frog celebrate its birthday?

During leap year!

Q: What's the difference between a new penny and an old nickel?

A: Four cents!

How did the skunk call his friend?

On a SMELL phone!

What's the difference between a cat and a flea?

A cat can have a flea, but a flea can't have a cat!

Author Antics!

A Call for Help
By Hugh Rang

Life Gave Me Lemons
By Maude Lemonade

Everybody Needs Affection
By Jimmy A. Hugg

Learning Not to Be Late
By Avery Time

How to Get Rich by Doing Nothing
By Candice B. Real

Making New Companions
By Anita Friend

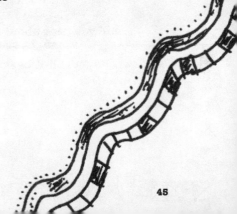

Just for the Pun of It!

Bernie: What year are baby chicks born in?

Ernie: Peep year!

Did you hear about the ear of corn that was caught speeding?

He got pulled over by a cob car!

Q: Did you hear about the drink of tea that got caught speeding?

A: He got pulled over by a cup car! ROTFL!

Stu: Did you hear about the chicken that was caught speeding?

Lou: She got pulled over by a coop car!

Did you hear about the dog that was caught speeding?

He got pulled over by the pup-lice!

Funny Bones

What did the giraffe doctor say to her waiting patients?

Necks! :P

Little Eva: What do you get when you cross a black dog with a white dog?

Big Eva: A greyhound!

Did you hear about the broken teacup that belonged to a duck?

It has a quack! HAR-DE-HAR-HAR-HAR!

Why did the duck get sent to the principal's office?

For using fowl language!

Griffin: Why do you have a banana in your ear?

Grace: I couldn't find my bicycle!

I Need a Good Laugh!

What does it say on the tombstone of a robot?

Rust in peace! LOL!

DEEP THOUGHTS: You can tune a piano, but you can't tuna fish!

Art student: I've been looking everywhere, but I can't find the glue!

Art teacher: Stick to it!

Q: How do you spell best friend with three letters?

A: D-O-G

Why did the kid bring a jump rope to school?

The teacher said she was doing good and could skip the math test!

Harry: What did the mollusk bring to its teacher?

Mary: A crab apple!

Going Bananas!

Mom: Why did the girl take a ladder to school?

Dad: She was going to HIGH school!

Why did the cake go to the doctor?

She was feeling crummy! LOL!

Teacher: Spell Delaware!
Student: The state or the river?

Hip: How was your math test?

Hop: The questions were easy!

Hip: Yay!

Hop: Yeah, but the answers were hard!

Mirthful Mix-Ups!

Kid: I'm glad you named me Grace!

Parent: Why?

Kid: Because that's what the teacher calls me!

How does a dog call his friends?

On a cell bone! ;)

Bill: What game do racecars like to play?

Jill: Hide and sleek!

Q: Why did the firefighter quit their job?

A: He was burned out!

Did you hear the joke about the stinkbug?

It really stunk!

Hank: Why was the cow a lousy dancer?

Frank: She had two left feet!

Ha-Ha's!

What does it say on the tombstone of a jigsaw puzzle?

Rest in pieces!

> **Q:** What does the stoplight do when it's embarrassed?
> **A:** It turns red!

What's black and white and red all over?

An embarrassed zebra!

> **Clara:** What did the farmer say when the last cow mooed good night?
>
> **Nett:** Now I've HERD everything.

Lol Library

Good Things to Put on Pizza
By Anne Chovies

How to Be a Plumber
By Leah King

Honey from Your Backyard
By B. Keeper

Fun at Camp
By Rhoda Horse

Try Hard and Succeed
By Willie Makit

Starting Conversations
By Howard U. Doing

Discovering Musical Talent
By Connie Singh

Do Be Silly!

Larry: Why did the gardener go to the library?

Gary: He wanted to WEED a good book!

Q: Which animal has its eyes closest together?
A: The smallest!

A mosquito bit me on the finger!

Which one?

I don't know. They're so small I can't tell one mosquito from another!

Restaurant owner: How do the customers like our new breakfast item?

Waiter: Great! It's selling like hotcakes! LOL!

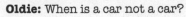

Oldie: When is a car not a car?

Goodie: When it turns into a garage! :D

Lotsa Laughs!

What drives a yellow car and lives in the ocean?

A CRAB driver!

When is a hole not a hole?

When it's a KNOT hole!

Evan: Why did the fork stop being friends with the knife?

Devin: He was always making cutting remarks!

She: What would you do if you saw a bluebird?

He: Make him happy by telling him a joke!

Daffy Laffy!

Q: What food do you eat when getting a makeover?
A: SPA-ghetti.

Hal: How do you like your new job as a carpet cleaner?

Al: It's RUG-ged!

Jenny: How do you like your job as a carpet installer?

Benny: I like it. I'm always laying down on the job!

Griffin: I swallowed a kazoo in music class!

School nurse: Good thing you weren't playing the tuba!

Moe: What do you get when you cross a cow with a rooster?

Joe: I don't know, but it says, "Cock-a-doodle-MOO!"

Q: Why couldn't the bicycle go up the hill?
A: Because it was TWO-TIRED!

Why did the farmer win the award?

Because she was outstanding in her field!

Why did the tree branch go to the doctor?
It was feeling STICK! :D

Lon: Why did the tennis racket lift weights?

Juan: He wanted to get STRUNG! LOL!

What's black and white and black and white and back and white?

A penguin rolling down a mountain!

What do bears use in their hair?

Bear spray.

Why did the bookcase get shhhh'ed in the library?

It was loudly talking to its shelf!

Q: Why was the blueberry late to the meeting?
A: He was in a traffic jam! HAHA!

Why did no one believe the boy after lunch?

He was full of baloney!

What kinds of pancakes go to gymnastics?
FLIP-jacks!

ROTFL!

Moe: What was the snail doing on the highway?

Joe: Ten feet an hour!

First astronomer: I don't know where the Dog Star is!
Second Astronomer: Are you SIRIUS?

Q: Why was the apple lonely?

A: The banana split! :P

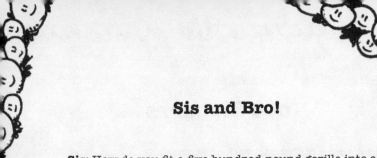

Sis and Bro!

Sis: How do you fit a five hundred-pound gorilla into a pencil box?

Bro: I dunno, how?

Sis: Take out the pencils!

Sis: How do you fit a two thousand-pound rhinoceros into a pencil box?

Bro: I dunno, how?!

SIS: Take out the five hundred-pound gorilla!!

Sis: How do you fit a six thousand-pound elephant into a pencil box?

Bro: I know! I know! Take out the two thousand-pound rhinoceros!!

SIS: NO WAY!!! A SIX THOUSAND-POUND ELEPHANT DOES NOT FIT INTO A PENCIL BOX!!!!!

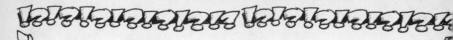

Knee Slappers

I just saw a materwityew!

What's a materwityew?!

Nothing really. What's the matter with you?!

> **Moe:** Doctor, can you see any change in me?
>
> **Joe:** No, why?
>
> **Moe:** I swallowed two dimes and a nickel!

Q: Why are clouds so high in the sky?

A: So giraffes don't bump their heads!

What do you do when you get a puzzle for your birthday?

Go to pieces! :D

Rock: Who's purple and an ancient Greek king?

Roll: Alexander the GRAPE!

Jim: Jolly Jack just drank juice from a jug in jail! How many Js in all?

June: Zilch! There are no Js in "all"!!!

What's green and has two wheels?

A motor-PICKLE! ROTFL!

What's purple and square?

An apple going incognito!

Why was Snow White a better soccer player than Cinderella?

Cinderella ran away from the ball!

Addled Addition!

Hairdressers + bakery = Do's and donuts!

Tremors + duck = Earth-quack!

Cracked teacup + ballerina = Break dancer!

Magician + big rig driver = Magic trucks!

Snowstorm + shark = Frost bite!

Hog + karate = Pork chop!

Parrot + piranha = I don't know, but it will talk your ear off!

Riddle Me This!

Tu: Thanks for giving me the alarm clock for my birthday!

Fro: Sure. Have a good time!

> **Q:** Where did the boat go when he was feeling sick?
>
> **A:** To the DOCK-tor!

What does the sign say on the door of chicken coop?

HEN-ter here!

Laugh Your Head Off!

Jack: Why was the mailbox damp inside?

Zack: The bills were DEW! LOL!

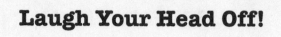

Why did the kangaroo tell her kids when she got tickled?

Go play outside!

Why couldn't the chicken play?

She had to study for her EGGS-ams!

Q: Why did the snowman marry the snowwoman?

A: It was love at FROST sight! :P

What instrument did the toothbrush play in band?

The TUBA-toothpaste!

What kind of riddles do marathoners tell?

Running jokes! ROTFL!

Animal Antics!

What looks like half a cow?

The other half!

What should you do if you feel like a dog?

SIT!

Q: Why is a giraffe tall and yellow with a tail?

A: Because if was short, green, and had wings it would be a parrot!

What did the pig comedian tell?

Corny jokes!

Jest Kidding!

I can't stop myself from going camping every weekend!

You're too intense! (In tents!)

> **How many stinkbugs does it take to make a bad smell?**
>
> Quite a PHEW! :D

Why did Alfred bring his stinkbug collection to school?

For show and SMELL!

Laffy Daffy!

What's smaller than flea's nose?

The hair on a flea's nose!

Honey: What did the wall say to the window?

Bea: You give me a PANE!

What did the waist say to the hula-hoop?

Get around these parts much? :D

Q: What invention enables you to walk through brick walls?

A: A door! LOL!

Tickle! Tickle!

Why did the pizza shop owner retire early?

She had made a lot of DOUGH!

She: What can you hold in your left hand but not in your right?

He: Your right elbow! LOL!

What do you get when you cross a five hundred-pound gorilla with a dog?

A nervous mail carrier!

What do kings and queens like to drink?

ROYAL-tea!

Willy: Please put this refrigerator on my credit card!

Nilly: I'm afraid your credit card is too small!

Belly Laughs!

How did the banana win the race?
He ran faster than all the other bananas!

What do you do when an apple tire goes flat?

You put on a pear tire!

What letter is always starting something?
S!

What did a Dalmatian say after eating dinner?

That hit the spots!

Floor: You don't look so good!
Escalator: I'm coming down with something!

Moe: Do you like my new shoes?
Joe: I didn't see them. Run them by me again!

Craig: How'd you get the kids to sleep?

Clizia: I just read them a few of the jokes in this book!

What's gray with big ears and has a trunk?

A mouse pirate! LOL!

So Funny I Remembered to Laugh!

Bill: I like to scratch my dog!

Jill: You're being PET-ty!

Q: Why did the steam kettle quit their job?
A: It couldn't stand the pressure!

How do chickens coax their chicks out of their shells?

They EGG them on!

Lou: I want to offer you the job of piloting my helicopter!

Stu: I'll take you up on that offer!

Why did the orange go to the doctor?

Because he wasn't PEEL-ing well!

WE ARE SORRY
THAT THIS PAGE
IS UPSIDE DOWN!
WE APOLOGISE
FOR THE ERROR!
-The Editor

Ha-larious!

Jim: I'm going to write my school report on the Sun!

Tim: That's a bright idea!

What's black and white and spins around?

A zebra going through a revolving door!

What the sound when a pig bumps its head?

B-OINK!

What's a monkey's favorite cookie?

Chocolate CHIMP!

What's the difference between a toasted breakfast cereal and an elderly farm animal with a beard?

One is a gold oat and the other is an old goat!

What the difference between a rock that fell off of a mountain and a portable device for communication?

One is a fell stone the other is a cell phone!

What is the difference between a highway in a valley and a canoe with six passengers!

One is a low road the other is a rowed load!

What's the difference between a stop signal and good parade?

One is a red light and the other is led right.

***

What do you get when you cross a five hundred-pound gorilla with a parrot?

I don't know!

Me neither, but you'd better listen!

Why did the cab driver get thrown in jail?

She took someone for a ride!

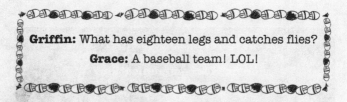

Griffin: What has eighteen legs and catches flies?

Grace: A baseball team! LOL!

What eats apples and wears a blue-and-white-striped uniform?

A worm that plays for the New York Yankees!

Where do you find red wood forests?

Wherever you left them.

Jest for Funzies!

Mom: Do you like your new math teacher?

Griffin: Yes, but she has a lot of problems!

Dad: Grace, do you like your new geology teacher?

Grace: Yes, but he has rocks in his head!

How do you make a five hundred-pound gorilla laugh?

You tickle him!

Q: How did the lighthouse keeper get her job?

A: She had friends in high places!

How did a watch become a quarterback?

Time passes!

What is the difference between a beige suit and a big chimney sweep?

One is a brown suit the other is a soot brute!

What's the difference between a speedy automobile and a baseball thrown from way out in the outfield?

One is a fast car the other is cast far!

What is the difference between a dog with floppy long ears and a pig with a broken leg?

One is a hound dog the other is a downed hog!

What is the difference between a rose-colored cap and a leader of rodents?

One is a red hat the other is a head rat!

Funzies!

What do you always overlook?

Your nose!

> **Sal:** I'm going to be in a marathon!
> **Hal:** You'll win in the long run!

Teacher: If you multiplied 4,876 by 6,345 what would you get?

Student: The wrong answer!

What's the difference between a five hundred-pound gorilla and a kitten?

You'll know the difference if a five hundred-pound gorilla sits on your lap!

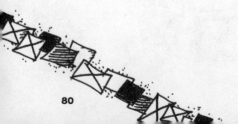

Look! A Book!

How to Keep from Forgetting
By Nora Idea

How to Enjoy School
By Olive Tulern

Can't We All Just Get Along?
By Les Try

Murder Mystery
By E. Dunit!

You Can Jump over Hurdles!
By Claire DeWay

Window Repair
By Douglas Brokin

Saying Good-Bye to Trouble
By Althea Later

Stop Being Negative
By Ron Thinking

Taking Night Classes
By Daisy Sleeps

Funny You Should Say That!

Why do anteaters not wear shoes, but only their socks?

So they can sneak up on ants!

Why do teachers wear sunglasses?

Because their students are so bright!

Larry: What's a cartoon?

Mary: A song you hear on the car radio!

Why was the skyscraper laughing?

He had many funny stories!

What do you say to an angry snowman?

Chill out!

Would you lie to join Robin Hood's merry men?

Sure would! (Sherwood!)

Did You Hear This One?!

Tim: Why did the man throw the clock
out the window?

Jim: He wanted to see time fly!

Lilly: What time is it when a six hundred-pound rhinoceros gets in your bed?

Billy: Time to get a new bed!!

**What did the chicken say when she
laid a square egg?**

Yee-outch!!!

What did the candle say when she had to go to the birthday party?

I have to GLOW now!

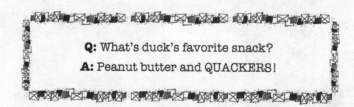

Q: What's duck's favorite snack?

A: Peanut butter and QUACKERS!

Your Side Will Ache!

What do turtles put on their bathroom floors?

REP-tiles!

What's the difference between a five hundred-pound gorilla and a cupcake?

A cupcake doesn't weigh five hundred pounds!

What insects aren't good football player?

FUMBLE bees!

Why did the candle fail its test?

It wasn't very bright!

Why did the goat write riddle books?

He was a big KID-der!

Author Antics

What's for Dinner?!
By Mac Incheez

Exciting Mystery Stories
By Paige Turner

Games at School
By Jim Nazium

Meals in a Jiffy
By Mike Roe Wave

Yummy Desserts
By E. Clair

This Is the Greatest Book in the World
By I. M. Serius

The Unfinished Book
By Adaline Moore

Animal Adds

Cow + lawnmower = lawnmooer

Turtle + basketball = snapshot!

Frog + snake = jump rope!

Cow + trampoline = milkshake

Cow + camel = lumpy milkshakes

Need Money?

Ask a skunk, it can give you a SCENT!

Ask a goat, it can you a BUCK!

Ask a duck, it can give you a BILL!

Ask a polar bear, it can give you cold hard cash!

Ask a horse, it can give you a HOOF-dollar!

Ask a cow, it can give you some MOO-la!

Ask a dog, it can give you a five-spot!

About the Author

Vice magazine has called Yoe the "Indiana Jones of comics historians." *Publisher Weekly* says he's the "archivist of the ridiculous and the sublime" and calls his work "brilliant." *The Onion* calls him a "celebrated designer," *The Library Journal* says, "a comics guru." BoingBoing hails him "a fine cartoonist and a comic book historian of the first water." Yoe was creative director/vice president/general manager of Jim Henson's Muppets, and a creative director at Nickelodeon and Disney. Craig has won an Eisner Award and the Gold Medal from the Society of Illustrators. Yoe has the record for writing and illustrating more kids' joke books than anyone on the planet.

Mango Publishing, established in 2014, publishes an eclectic list of books by diverse authors—both new and established voices—on topics ranging from business, personal growth, women's empowerment, LGBTQ studies, health, and spirituality to history, popular culture, time management, decluttering, lifestyle, mental wellness, aging, and sustainable living. We were recently named 2019's #1 fastest growing independent publisher by Publishers Weekly. Our success is driven by our main goal, which is to publish high quality books that will entertain readers as well as make a positive difference in their lives.

Our readers are our most important resource; we value your input, suggestions, and ideas. We'd love to hear from you—after all, we are publishing books for you!

Please stay in touch with us and follow us at:

Facebook: Mango Publishing
Twitter: @MangoPublishing
Instagram: @MangoPublishing
LinkedIn: Mango Publishing
Pinterest: Mango Publishing

Sign up for our newsletter at www. mangopublishinggroup.com and receive a free book!

Join us on Mango's journey to reinvent publishing, one book at a time.

CPSIA information can be obtained
at www.ICGtesting.com
Printed in the USA
LVHW031118221220
674795LV00002B/2